NUTRITION AND
YOUR BODY

YOUR BODY ON SUGAR

BY ANITA YASUDA

CONTENT CONSULTANT
Steven C. Fordahl, PhD
Assistant Professor, Department of Nutrition
University of North Carolina at Greensboro

Core Library

An Imprint of Abdo Publishing
abdobooks.com

Cover image: Doughnuts are one of many sources
of sugar.

abdocorelibrary.com

Published by Abdo Publishing, a division of ABDO, PO Box 398166, Minneapolis, Minnesota 55439. Copyright © 2020 by Abdo Consulting Group, Inc. International copyrights reserved in all countries. No part of this book may be reproduced in any form without written permission from the publisher. Core Library™ is a trademark and logo of Abdo Publishing.

Printed in the United States of America, North Mankato, Minnesota
012019
092019

THIS BOOK CONTAINS
RECYCLED MATERIALS

Cover Photo: Shutterstock Images
Interior Photos: Shutterstock Images, 1, 6, 12–13, 25; iStockphoto, 4–5, 15, 16–17, 22–23, 26–27, 29 (soda), 29 (muffin), 29 (cereal), 34–35, 43, 45; Joe Belanger/iStockphoto, 9; Vladislav Klok/iStockphoto, 19; Cansu Demirsoy/Shutterstock Images, 29 (doughnut); AMR Image/iStockphoto, 31; Dennis Kunkel Microscopy/Science Photo Library/Alamy, 36; Rich Legg/iStockphoto, 40

Editor: Marie Pearson
Series Designer: Claire Vanden Branden

Library of Congress Control Number: 2018964507

Publisher's Cataloging-in-Publication Data

Names: Yasuda, Anita, author.
Title: Your body on sugar / by Anita Yasuda
Description: Minneapolis, Minnesota : Abdo Publishing, 2020 | Series: Nutrition and your body | Includes online resources and index.
Identifiers: ISBN 9781532118876 (lib. bdg.) | ISBN 9781532173059 (ebook) | ISBN 9781644940785 (pbk.)
Subjects: LCSH: Sugars--Physiological effect--Juvenile literature. | Sugar in the body--Juvenile literature. | Blood sugar--Juvenile literature. | Food--Health aspects--Juvenile literature.
Classification: DDC 613.20--dc23

CONTENTS

MAR 2020

WHAT IS SUGAR?

Anya raced through the fair. She wanted to buy something to eat. The air was hot and smelled of fresh pretzels and kettle corn. Her stomach growled at her to hurry up.

Anya wandered by rows of pies and cakes. She could barely believe the size of the golden-brown funnel cakes topped with strawberries. She looked back at the ice cream sundaes and cones. Then she stopped to watch a person spin strands of sugar round and round. She took a big breath as it

Fairgoers can choose from all sorts of sweet treats.

began to look like a
pink fluffy cloud.

Her hand closed
over the money in her
pocket. She bought a
bag of the pink cotton
candy. The cloud was
as big as her head. It
melted in her mouth
when she took a bite. It
was very sweet.

Sugar made the
cotton candy sweet.
The sugar tickled the
taste buds on the tip
of Anya's tongue.

DIGESTION

The small intestine is an organ. It helps break down food into sugars. It looks like a long winding tube. In adults, it is approximately 22 feet (6.7 m) long. The tube is only a little wider than a thumb. Food spends up to four hours here. Millions of tiny blood vessels cover parts of the small intestine. They are found in part of the intestines called villi. Sugars enter the blood through the villi. Then the sugars are carried to every cell, where they become energy for the body.

She took another big bite. When she swallowed it, the
cotton candy slid down into her stomach. It stopped

Cotton candy is almost entirely made of sugar.

there and in her small intestine, where it was mixed and mashed. The sugar moved into her blood. A wave of energy zipped all around her body, but only for a short time. She soon wanted more sweet foods.

SWEET FOODS

Sugar is in everyday foods and drinks. Sugar is found naturally in many foods, such as raisins and cherry tomatoes. There is natural sugar in carrot sticks and apple slices. But some sweet-tasting foods have sugar added to them.

Sodas and candy have a lot of sugar. People add sugar to muffins and cereals. It makes food look and taste good. Sugar in treats such as cookies makes them crispy. Sugar helps meat stay fresh longer. Some foods with sugar do not taste very sweet at all. There is sugar in many pasta sauces, soups, and breads. Approximately 68 percent of all packaged food sold in grocery stores has sugar.

Sugar gives fruits their sweetness.

If you could look at sugar under a powerful microscope, you would see that it is made up of tiny building blocks. These blocks are called elements. They are carbon, hydrogen, and oxygen. These three elements are the building blocks of carbohydrates. Carbohydrates are nutrients, or substances the body

SENSE OF TASTE

The sense of taste allows a person to enjoy sweet apples, salty chips, sour plums, and bitter olives. When a person eats, tiny bumps on the tongue taste the food. Approximately 10,000 of these taste buds coat the top and sides of the tongue. Each bump has taste sensors. The sensors send messages about the food to the brain, where they are read. A person uses this information to tell if a food is fresh or if a food has gone bad. A person can also tell what type of nutrients, especially sugar, are in the food.

needs to stay well. Along with protein and fat, carbohydrates are one of the three main nutrients in your food. Carbohydrates make up approximately 60 percent of our daily food. Sugar is a carbohydrate. Starch and fiber are also carbohydrates.

The body must break down carbohydrates to get at the energy in food. This process happens in the digestive system. During digestion, carbohydrates become smaller and smaller units of sugar. The body uses this sugar as energy. Everything the body does needs energy. The body uses energy to grow and breathe. It uses energy to read, talk, and run. However, sugars are not all the same. They have different effects on the body. Knowing more about how sugars work and in which foods to find them is a great way to stay healthy and strong.

FURTHER EVIDENCE

Chapter One describes why people like sugar and how the body digests it. Why do people like sugar? What examples support this point? Read the information on the website below. Find a quote from the website that supports this information. What new evidence does it present?

NATIONAL PUBLIC RADIO: THE GENE FOR SWEET
abdocorelibrary.com/sugar

CHAPTER
TWO

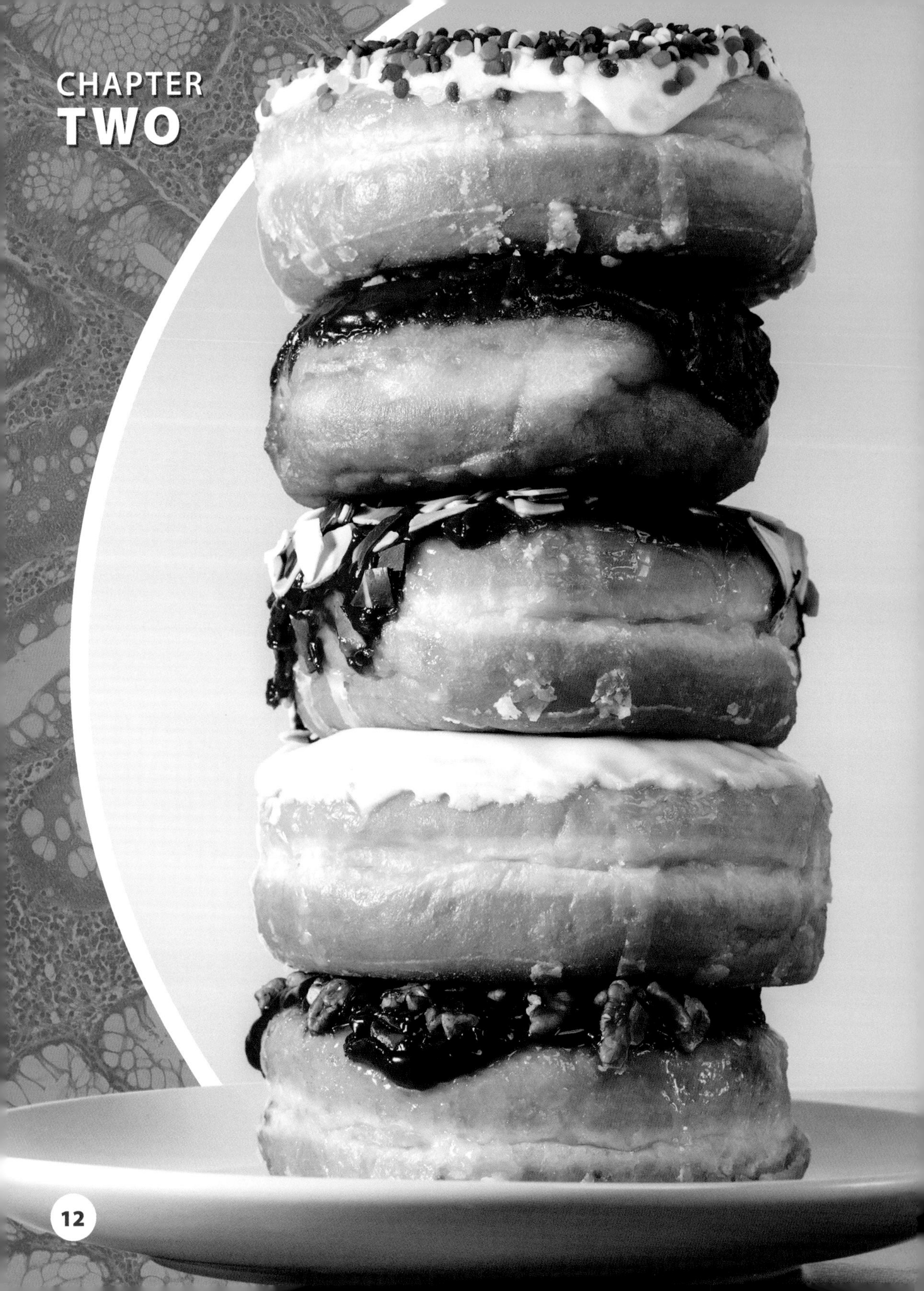

SOURCES OF SUGAR

Many of the foods people eat are high in added sugar. Added sugars are not a natural part of foods. Most of the added sugar that people eat is sucrose. Sucrose is also known as table sugar, or it may simply be called sugar. Sucrose comes from plants.

Sunflowers, marigolds, and pine trees make sugar. In fact, all green plants make sugar using light from the sun. They turn this light into energy in the photosynthesis process. *Photo* means "light," and *synthesis* means "to put together." Plants trap light in their leaves. They also use their leaves to take in a gas

Pastries such as doughnuts are high in added sugar.

13

THE STEVIA PLANT

There are plant-based sweeteners in processed foods. They taste sweet, but they are not sugar. Stevia is a plant that grows in areas of South America. It is naturally sweet, but it is not sugar. The plant is up to 450 times sweeter than sugar. Indigenous peoples have been using the plant for hundreds of years. The Guarani people of Paraguay use stevia in tea. The plant was not known outside South America until the 1500s. This is when Spanish scientist Pedro Jamie Esteve learned of it. Today, stevia is a popular sweetener because people can bake and cook with it. They use it in ice cream, yogurt, sodas, and iced tea. It has almost no calories.

called carbon dioxide from the air. This is the gas that people and animals breathe out. Plant roots take in water from the soil.

A plant takes apart the carbon dioxide and water molecules. Then, it can rearrange them into sugar molecules. Plants can use this sugar to grow. They also store some in their roots, flowers, or seeds. Most plants make just enough sugar to stay strong or last them over a winter. Two plants make so

Sugar beets store sugar in their roots.

much sugar that people can harvest it. They are sugar cane and sugar beets.

TABLE SUGAR

More than 120 countries produce sugar. Approximately 80 percent of this sugar comes from sugar cane. The rest is from sugar beets. Brazil grows more sugar

Sugar cane's stalks hold sugar.

cane than any other country. In the United States, sugar cane grows in Florida, Louisiana, and Texas.

Sugar cane is a giant grass that can grow as high as 13 feet (4 m) tall. The top of the plant is green and fluffy. Its narrow stem looks like a long tube. About 12 to 16 months after planting, the sugar cane is cut down. Mills turn the stems into sugar crystals. One hundred

and ten short tons (100 metric tons) of sugar cane make up to 11 short tons (10 metric tons) of raw sugar.

The second major source of table sugar comes from sugar beets. A sugar beet seed is no larger than a peppercorn. The seed grows into a green leafy plant with thick white roots. The plant's sugar is in these roots. For centuries, people only ate the beet greens. It wasn't

NUTRITION LABELS

Labels on food list the amount of nutrients in one serving. People can use labels as a tool. When they read the list of ingredients, they can make wiser choices about what they eat and buy. By 2021, food labels in the United States must list all added sugars. But there are more than 152 ways to say sugar on a label. Sometimes the word *sugar* is in the name of the ingredient. This is true for things such as brown sugar or date sugar. Often these names do not have the word *sugar* in them. Names ending in *-ose*, such as fructose and glucose, are often sugars.

until 1747 that chemist Andreas Sigismund Marggraf found a way to make sugar from beets. Juice from the beets is heated until it becomes a thick syrup. As the liquid cools, sugar crystals form. These white crystals are sucrose.

TYPES OF ADDED SUGAR

Fruits such as dates are also sources of added sugar. People take the sugars from these fruits and add them to other foods. Maple sap and honey are naturally sweet. They can also be used as added sugars. Sap flows

SUGAR IN FRUITS AND VEGETABLES

FRUIT OR VEGETABLE	GRAMS OF SUGAR PER SERVING
Apples	25g
Broccoli	2g
Carrots	5g
Grapes	20g
Strawberries	8g
Sweet Corn	5g

All fruits and vegetables contain sugar. These levels vary depending on the fruit or vegetable. Look closely at the chart. Select one fruit and one vegetable from it. How many times a week do you eat these foods? Can you think of other ways to add more fruits and vegetables to your diet?

from a sugar maple tree in the spring. It takes more than 30 gallons (115 L) of sap to make one gallon (4 L) of syrup. Honey comes from nectar collected by honeybees. It takes more than 500 honeybees to gather one pound (0.5 kg) of honey from flowers. Honey and syrup are used in snack bars and teas. Another liquid sweetener is high-fructose corn syrup (HFCS). It is made from cornstarch and costs less than table sugar to make. Some jams, cereals, and sodas use HFCS as a cheaper alternative to sugar.

There are also artificial sweeteners in our food. They are made of chemicals that copy the taste of sugar. They may be found in soda, pudding, candy, and jam. They have few or no carbohydrates or calories. They are also many times sweeter than table sugar. Some, such as saccharin, are approximately 500 times sweeter than sugar. Many people choose to eat foods with artificial sweeteners. This is because the food has fewer calories. However, scientists do not know if artificial sweeteners are better for the body than table sugar. They are still studying the effects on the body.

STRAIGHT TO THE
SOURCE

Marlene Schwartz, director of the University of Connecticut Rudd Center for Food Policy and Obesity, describes why it is a good idea to not sell chocolate milk in schools:

> *Why is it that when [children] enter kindergarten, suddenly we think oh, no, they're not going to like [plain milk] anymore and we introduce something that's significantly higher in sugar and calories? . . .*
>
> *What we found in our research, is essentially children drink what's served. And so, sure, if you put chocolate milk next to plain milk, a lot of children will choose the chocolate milk. Of course they will, because it's higher in sugar and it tastes sweeter. I think the key is to really promote the drinks that you want them to be consuming.*
>
> Source: "Chocolate Milk: Good or Bad for Kids?" *Tell Me More.* NPR, November 11, 2009. Web. Accessed October 15, 2018.

Changing Minds

Imagine you are taking part in a debate at school. Your teacher has asked you to argue whether or not chocolate milk should be banned at school. How might you use the information above to support your point?

SUGAR AND HEALTH

The sugars in carbohydrates are part of a good diet. There are two types of carbohydrates: simple and complex. Some simple carbohydrates are made of only one type of sugar molecule. These sugar molecules are called monosaccharides. They are the simplest forms of carbohydrates. Fructose, glucose, and galactose are monosaccharides.

Honey is so sweet with monosaccharides that it is often used to sweeten other foods.

Monosaccharides make foods such as honey and fruit sweet.

Often, two types of sugar molecules pair up. They become a disaccharide. In milk, a molecule each of glucose and galactose pair up. They form the disaccharide lactose. Disaccharides are the more common form of simple carbohydrates in nature. They are also the most common form of added sugar.

A complex carbohydrate has three or more types of sugar molecules linked together. The starch in rice or pasta is a complex carbohydrate. Starch has long sugar chains. Some chains have as many as 1,000 sugar molecules.

The body absorbs the sugar in simple and complex carbohydrates at different speeds. The sugar in a cookie enters the blood quickly. As blood sugar levels rise, the body makes insulin. This chemical moves the sugar into the cells that need it. The sugar does not make people hyper. But they do feel a charge of energy as their sugar

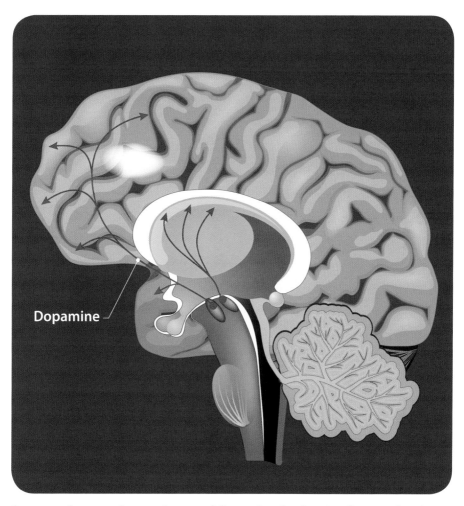

Dopamine

Sugar releases dopamine, *red lines*, in the brain. Dopamine is a chemical that controls pleasure.

levels rise. This rush of energy does not last long. A few hours later, people usually feel tired.

In contrast, the body takes longer to absorb the sugar in a complex carbohydrate. This is because foods

Pasta may not taste as sweet as honey or fruit. But it still contains sugar.

such as bread have more starch. The body must break down this starch into sugar before it can enter the cells. Blood sugar levels do not rise as much. The body has energy longer.

Simple sugars are not always unhealthy. They appear naturally in many foods such as fruits. Fruits typically also have lots of fiber. The body cannot digest fiber. Fiber slows down how quickly the body digests simple sugars. So the sugar doesn't damage the body. However, fruit juice is different from whole fruits. The parts with fiber have been removed. So drinking fruit juice is like drinking a soda. The body absorbs the sugar quickly. This causes large blood sugar swings. These swings are hard on the body.

FEELING GOOD

Scientists have found that sugar can trick the brain into wanting more food. When people eat sugar, the brain releases the chemical dopamine. This chemical makes people feel good. It also affects how they eat. Because eating sugar makes people feel happy, they want to eat more. But when people eat too much sugar, the brain can get used to it. Over time, it takes more sugar to create the same good feeling. People can gain weight as they take in more food than they should.

HEALTH PROBLEMS

The average American diet is full of added sugars. Added sugars can be monosaccharides or disaccharides. In the 1800s, people had approximately 10 teaspoons (49 ml) of sugar every five days.

SUGAR IN SNACK FOODS

SNACK FOOD		SUGAR CONTENT
	Soft Drink	8 teaspoons (35g)
	Jelly Donut	3 teaspoons (14g)
	Muffin	6 teaspoons (24g)
	Sugar-Coated Cornflakes	3 teaspoons (13g)

The American Heart Association recommends children eat no more than 25 grams of added sugar each day. Look at the graph of the amount of sugar in some popular snacks. What does the graph tell you about how much added sugar you eat in your snacks? What foods with less sugar could you eat instead?

People now have this much every seven hours. Many doctors worry about this increase. A diet high in sugars can raise blood fats. These fats are known as triglycerides. They build up on the walls of blood vessels. Over time, this can cut off the blood flow.

READY, CHECK

People with diabetes work hard to keep their blood sugar levels healthy. They need to check their levels each day. They can test their levels with a small machine called a glucose meter. Pricking a finger to draw a drop of blood is the first step. A small strip then catches the drop of blood. The machine checks the sample. Within seconds, the meter displays a number. Based on this number, people know how much insulin or food they need to balance their levels.

Then, a heart attack can happen. Each year, more than 700,000 people have a heart attack in the United States.

Another risk of eating too much sugar is obesity. When people have more body fat than is healthy, they are said to be obese. In the United States, this disease affects 20 percent of children ages 6 to 19. Children with obesity are also more likely to get type 2 diabetes. Diabetes is a disease in which the body does not make enough insulin, or the cells do not use insulin as they should. Extra fat can reduce the

People with diabetes may need to test their blood sugar levels with a special device.

effectiveness of insulin. When the body cannot move sugar into cells, it can suffer organ damage. More than 5,000 children develop diabetes each year. Doctors suggest that people eat less sugar to keep a healthy weight. Getting enough exercise is also important.

BRAIN POWER

Sugar helps the brain work well. The brain fuels up its neurons, or nerve cells, with sugar. The neurons carry messages back and forth all over the body. The brain can then control everything the body does. It tells the heart to pump blood. It tells the lungs to breathe. It also tells the body when it needs to eat. The brain uses sugar in the blood for energy. It uses more energy than any other organ. Approximately 60 percent of all sugar in the blood goes to the brain.

Thinking, memory, and learning are also linked to sugar levels. Some studies found that sugar may help students before a test. It gives them a quick boost of energy. But too much sugar over a long time may be bad for the brain. A 2017 study looked at the link between eating sugar and memory. More than 4,000 people took part in the study. Most people who had sugary drinks did worse on the memory test. But the full impact of sugar on memory is not yet clear. There is still a lot more to be learned.

STRAIGHT TO THE
SOURCE

Associate professor of applied nutrition Jess Haines describes how spikes in blood sugar can be avoided:

The body's response to sugar can be altered by a number of factors, including the foods that are eaten with the sugary treat. Eating a sugary treat along with foods high in protein or fibre can result in a smaller rise in blood sugar. To reduce their child's spike in blood sugar, parents should resist the urge to pack a Halloween treat in their children's lunch where they will be unable to control what is eaten with it. Instead, parents can allow their children a treat after the dinner meal, where the children can be more closely monitored. If followed by a good teeth brushing, parents can also reduce their child's risk of cavities.

Source: Jess Haines. "How to Avoid a Halloween Sugar Disaster." *The Conversation*. The Conversation, October 30, 2017. Web. Accessed September 20, 2018.

Consider Your Audience

Review this passage closely. Imagine that you are going to write a blog post for your friends about how they can eat their treats in a way that is healthier for their bodies. How will you present the information contained in the passage on your blog? How is your approach different from the original article and why?

SUGAR AND TEETH

Some people think that teeth are bones because both are hard and white. But bones are living tissue. This means the cells within bones can grow and mend themselves. Not all parts of teeth have living tissue. Like your fingernails and hair, the outer layer of teeth does not have living cells. This layer is the enamel. It is the hardest part of the body. Under the enamel is the soft living tissue, dentin. Next is the pulp, where the nerves and blood vessels are.

Teeth are strong, but they also need to be cared for. This is because a crack or decay

Knowing what foods do the most damage to teeth can help people keep their teeth healthy.

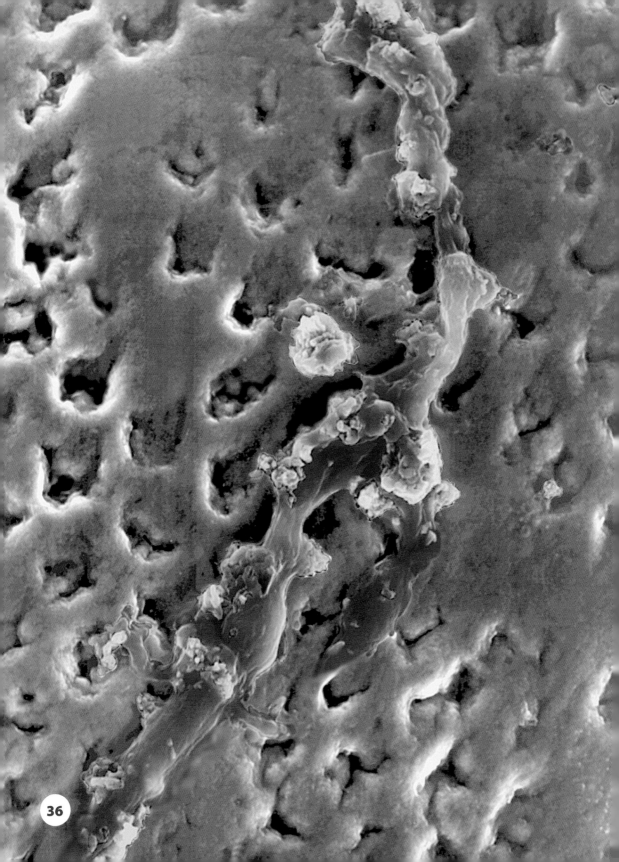

can let bacteria enter the tooth. Bacteria are too small to see without a microscope. But they are always in the mouth. There are as many as 300 types of bacteria in the mouth. Some bacteria protect the teeth. But some take part in tooth decay. Cavity-causing bacteria feed on sugars and starches. People who eat food high in sugar can have more dental problems than people who do not.

HUNGRY BACTERIA

Bacteria change sugar into an acid as they feed. This acid is so strong that it can eat away at tooth enamel. But the mouth has a defense against this acid. The saliva in your mouth makes the acid weaker. Saliva also has enzymes that kill some of the bacteria.

However, if a person keeps eating foods high in sugar, the bacteria keeps growing. Small white spots may form on the teeth. The spots are a sign that the enamel is breaking down. The teeth cannot fix

A magnified image shows bacteria buildup, *green areas*, on a tooth.

SIP AND DECAY

Many everyday foods have low levels of acids. But soda has high amounts of sugar and acid that can damage teeth. It takes only five minutes for the acid in a soda to soften tooth enamel. Acid can be measured on a scale from 0 to 14. This scale is called the pH scale. The lower the number, the more acidic something is. Water is neutral with a pH of 7. Anything that is lower than 5.5 can harm your teeth. The average pH level in soda is below 4.

themselves. A dentist needs to fix them. If a tooth is left untreated, those white spots may turn black. They may become a hole or a cavity. The bacteria attack the pulp through the hole made by the acid. Infection can then spread through the blood to other parts of the body. Very rarely, people have even died when the bacteria reached their brain.

GOOD HABITS

In the United States, 42 percent of children have cavities in their baby teeth. To keep teeth healthy, dentists suggest a diet with less sugar. This way, the bacteria in the mouth will have less to live on. Brushing and flossing are also important. They help keep the mouth clean. A toothbrush can get rid of food on the teeth's surface, while flossing gets rid of food that may be stuck between the teeth. Rinsing with water can also help keep teeth clean. So can chewing sugarless gum. Chewing encourages the mouth to make more saliva. The acid level in the mouth then drops.

HEALTHY BODY

Keeping your body healthy does not mean giving up sugar. However, too much

SUPERHERO HEALTH

The American Academy of Pediatric Dentistry (AAPD) uses the internet to educate children about tooth decay and diet. In 2014, the AAPD created the Little Teeth League. They are a group of online superhero characters. These superheroes do not leap tall buildings, but they do teach kids how to care for their teeth. Kids also learn about the role of sugar in decay. The Little Teeth League includes Brushing Boy, Cavity Clasher, and the Flying Flosser. The team is always ready to fight off the monster Tooth D. K., who loves sugar.

People can enjoy sugar in small amounts and on special occasions and still be healthy.

sugar can lead to health problems. Healthy foods fuel your body with energy to play and learn. They can also help you feel better about yourself.

Instead of a sugary donut, add fresh fruit to unsweetened yogurt. Or munch on a whole-grain snack.

These foods can give you lots of nutrients and no added sugars. Most soda is full of sugar. You could swap out this drink with water or milk. You can also check a food item's nutrition label. This label will tell you how much added sugar the food has. One small sugar-smart decision a day can have a big impact on your health.

EXPLORE ONLINE

Chapter Four includes information about how sugar affects teeth. The video at the website below focuses on the same subject. As you know, every source is different. How is the information on this site different from what you have read in this chapter? How is it the same? What can you learn from this website about taking care of your teeth?

PBS: WHAT REALLY CAUSES CAVITIES?
abdocorelibrary.com/sugar

FAST FACTS

- Sugar is a source of energy.

- Sugars are molecules of carbon, hydrogen, and oxygen.

- The sugars glucose, fructose, and galactose are monosaccharides, the simplest form of carbohydrates and the building blocks of complex carbohydrates. When two monosaccharides pair up, they form disaccharides.

- Monosaccharides and disaccharides are found in a variety of foods and drinks such as fruit and milk. They are also used as added sugars.

- Added sugars are sugars and syrups added to foods such as cookies and soft drinks when they are made. They absorb quickly into the body.

- Complex carbohydrates, such as pasta and rice, have many sugars linked together. They absorb more slowly into the body, so the body has energy longer.

- Sugar is found in 68 percent of all packaged food sold in grocery stores.

- Eating large amounts of sugar may lead to weight gain and diseases such as diabetes.

- Sugar can cause dental cavities.

- The brain relies on sugar to function, but too much may affect memory.

STOP AND
THINK

Tell the Tale

Chapter One of this book begins with a girl at a fair. Imagine you are wandering through the same fair. Write 200 words describing the food at the fair. What food and drinks do you see? What do they look and smell like? What do you choose and why? Do any of your favorite fair foods contain sugar?

Surprise Me

Chapter Three discusses how your body uses sugar and the harm it can cause. After reading this book, what two or three facts about how the body uses sugar did you find most surprising? Write a few sentences about each fact. Why did you find each fact surprising?

Dig Deeper

After reading this book, what questions do you still have about sugar? With an adult's help, find a few reliable sources that can help you answer your questions. Write a paragraph about what you learned.

Say What?

Learning about sugar can mean learning a lot of new vocabulary. Find five words in this book you've never heard before. Use a dictionary to find out what they mean. Then write the meanings in your own words, and use each word in a new sentence.

GLOSSARY

bacteria
a type of single-celled organism, some of which can cause disease

digestive system
a group of organs that work together to turn food into fuel for the body

enzyme
a protein that helps break down food

fructose
a sugar molecule also called fruit sugar; found in fruits and honey

galactose
a sugar molecule found in dairy products

glucose
a sugar molecule found in fruits and vegetables that can be directly absorbed into the blood

insulin
a protein the body makes that travels in the blood, keeping sugar levels from getting too high

molecule
the smallest unit of a chemical compound

packaged food
a food that is frozen, canned, baked, or fried before being sold

sucrose
the sugar that comes from sugar cane or sugar beets that is turned into table sugar

ONLINE RESOURCES

To learn more about your body on sugar, visit our free resource websites below.

Visit **abdocorelibrary.com** or scan this QR code for free Common Core resources for teachers and students, including vetted activities, multimedia, and booklinks, for deeper subject comprehension.

Visit **abdobooklinks.com** or scan this QR code for free additional online weblinks for further learning. These links are routinely monitored and updated to provide the most current information available.

LEARN MORE

Burling, Alexis. *Your Body on Carbohydrates*. Minneapolis, MN: Abdo Publishing, 2020. Print.

Rissman, Rebecca. *Processed Foods*. Minneapolis, MN: Abdo Publishing, 2016. Print.

INDEX

About the Author

Anita Yasuda is the author of many books for young readers. Her children's book *Explore Simple Machines!* won the Society of School Librarians International Honor Book Award for science books, grades K–6, in 2012. Anita divides her time between both coasts.